Dope Thief

(Movie Review)

The Inspiration Behind the Film and What you should Know Before the Release

Douglas H. Hatcher

Table Of Contents

Introduction

The crime drama genre has long captivated audiences with its intense storytelling, complex characters, and high-stakes conflicts. With the upcoming release of *Dope Thief* on March 14, 2025, Apple TV+ is set to deliver another gripping entry into the world of crime thrillers. Based on the 2009 novel by Dennis Tafoya, this miniseries brings to life a story filled with deception, survival, and the consequences of one fateful decision.

This book serves as a comprehensive review of *Dope Thief*, examining its cinematic execution, narrative depth, and the performances that drive its story forward. From the background of the novel and its adaptation to the unique elements that set this series apart, readers will gain a thorough understanding of what makes this crime drama a must-watch. With insights into the cast, production details, and potential plot twists, this book will provide everything needed to appreciate *Dope Thief* beyond the screen. Whether you are a crime drama enthusiast or a casual viewer, this book offers a detailed analysis that enhances the viewing experience.

Overview of *Dope Thief*

Dope Thief is an American crime drama miniseries created by Peter Craig, set to premiere on Apple TV+ on March 14, 2025. The series follows two Philadelphia-based friends who pose as DEA agents to rob drug houses, only to find themselves entangled in a larger and more dangerous operation than they ever anticipated. With its foundation rooted in the gritty, morally complex storytelling of the original novel, *Dope Thief* explores themes of loyalty, survival, and the high price of deception.

The show stars Brian Tyree Henry as Ray, a man drawn into the world of crime by desperation and circumstance. Wagner Moura co-stars as Manny Carvalho, his partner in crime who brings his own set of skills and motivations to the duo's illegal activities. With additional performances by Marin Ireland, Kate Mulgrew, and Ving Rhames, the cast is filled with talent capable of bringing depth to this tense and atmospheric narrative.

What distinguishes *Dope Thief* from other crime dramas is its commitment to realism. Rather than relying on exaggerated action sequences, it focuses on the psychological turmoil of its protagonists and the ever-present tension that comes with living on the edge of the law. The show's cinematography, led by Erik Messerschmidt, ensures a raw and immersive experience, while Dominic Lewis's score intensifies the emotional and suspenseful beats of the story. As the series unfolds, audiences can expect a meticulously crafted crime drama that not only entertains but also provokes thought about the choices that lead individuals down irreversible paths.

Background on the Novel & Adaptation

The television adaptation of *Dope Thief* is rooted in the acclaimed crime novel of the same name by Dennis Tafoya, first published in 2009. The novel was praised for its fast-paced narrative, sharp dialogue, and deep exploration of flawed but compelling characters. Tafoya's work often focuses on individuals living on the fringes of society, and *Dope Thief* is no exception. It presents a raw and unflinching look at criminals who, despite their illegal actions, remain deeply human in their struggles and motivations.

Peter Craig, known for his work on *The Batman* and *Bad Boys for Life*, took on the challenge of adapting the novel for television. His experience in crafting dynamic, character-driven action stories made him a fitting choice for the project. Working alongside Ridley Scott as an executive producer, Craig sought to preserve the essence of the novel while making necessary adjustments to fit the episodic format.

One of the key differences between the novel and the miniseries lies in its visual storytelling. While the book relies on internal monologues and character introspection, the show translates these elements into expressive cinematography, nuanced performances, and a tightly woven script. Additionally, the adaptation expands on certain plot points, introducing new characters and deepening the backstories of Ray and Manny to enhance the audience's emotional connection to their journey.

With its faithful yet innovative approach to adaptation, *Dope Thief* is poised to honor the source material while offering fresh surprises for both longtime fans of the book and newcomers to the story.

What Makes This Crime Drama Unique

Dope Thief distinguishes itself from other crime dramas through its character-driven storytelling, grounded realism, and thematic depth. While crime thrillers often emphasize action and high-stakes heists, this series delves deeper into the psychological and emotional weight of its protagonists' choices.

One of the standout elements of *Dope Thief* is its exploration of identity and morality. Ray and Manny are not merely criminals; they are individuals shaped by their pasts, driven by desperation, and constantly forced to navigate the thin line between survival and self-destruction. The series challenges the audience to sympathize with characters who exist in morally ambiguous territory, making their journey all the more compelling.

The show's production values also contribute to its uniqueness. Erik Messerschmidt's cinematography captures the gritty and often claustrophobic environment of Philadelphia's underbelly, while Dominic Lewis's score amplifies the tension and emotional stakes. The decision to film on location further enhances the authenticity of the story, immersing viewers in a world that feels both real and unforgiving.

Another defining aspect of *Dope Thief* is its unpredictability. Unlike formulaic crime dramas that rely on familiar tropes, this series keeps viewers on edge with its unexpected character developments and plot twists. The moral dilemmas faced by Ray and Manny unfold in ways that defy easy resolutions, ensuring that the audience remains engaged from start to finish.

With its unique blend of psychological depth, intense storytelling, and stellar production quality, *Dope Thief* sets itself apart as a must-watch crime drama that offers far more than just high-stakes heists and action-packed sequences.

What Readers Can Expect from This Book

This book aims to serve as the ultimate companion to *Dope Thief*, offering an in-depth exploration of every aspect of the series. Readers can expect a thorough analysis of the show's themes, characters, and narrative structure, as well as behind-the-scenes insights into its production and adaptation process.

Each chapter is designed to provide a detailed perspective on the elements that make *Dope Thief* a standout crime drama. From examining the performances of its talented cast to uncovering hidden details within its cinematography and storytelling, this book will enrich the viewing experience for audiences who wish to go beyond surface-level entertainment.

This book will delve into the possible plot twists and character arcs that may shape the series' trajectory. By analyzing the source material and the creative choices made in the adaptation, readers will gain a deeper understanding of the story's underlying messages and potential directions.

Whether you are a fan of crime dramas, an admirer of well-crafted storytelling, or simply someone interested in learning more about the process of adapting literature to television, this book offers valuable insights that will enhance your appreciation of *Dope Thief.* With its comprehensive approach and engaging analysis, it serves as the perfect guide to one of the most highly anticipated crime dramas of 2025.

Chapter 1

The Cast & Characters

The success of a crime drama like *Dope Thief* is often tied to the strength of its cast. In this case, the performances of Brian Tyree Henry, Wagner Moura, and the supporting ensemble play a critical role in bringing the story to life. The casting choices reflect a commitment to authenticity, depth, and compelling storytelling. Each actor has been selected not only for their talent but also for their ability to embody the complexities of their characters.

Brian Tyree Henry takes on the role of Ray, a character central to the story's emotional and narrative core. Henry's past performances in films and television, particularly his work in *Atlanta*, have established him as an actor capable of bringing depth to morally complex roles. In *Dope Thief*, he portrays a man entangled in a world of crime, navigating the consequences of his choices with a combination of intelligence and desperation. His performance is expected to add a layer of authenticity that makes Ray a character audiences can empathize with, despite his morally ambiguous actions. Henry's ability to balance vulnerability and intensity makes him a fitting choice for the role.

Wagner Moura plays Manny Carvalho, a key figure in the unfolding drama. Moura is well known for his portrayal of Pablo Escobar in *Narcos*, a role that showcased his ability to portray both charm and menace. His character in *Dope Thief* is expected to bring a similar complexity, playing a man who is both an ally and a potential threat to Ray. The dynamic between Henry and Moura will be a defining feature of the series, shaping its tension and momentum. Their on-screen chemistry will be crucial in depicting the power struggles and shifting loyalties that drive the story forward.

Beyond the lead actors, the supporting cast adds depth and nuance to the series. Marin Ireland plays Mina, a character whose role in the narrative adds emotional weight and a different perspective on the central conflict. Ireland is known for her performances in *Hell or High*

Water and *Sneaky Pete*, where she has demonstrated an ability to bring complex, layered characters to life. In *Dope Thief*, she is likely to serve as a crucial figure who influences Ray's decisions and personal journey.

Kate Mulgrew, recognized for her work in *Star Trek: Voyager* and *Orange is the New Black*, plays Theresa Bowers. Her presence in the cast suggests a strong and authoritative character, potentially someone with significant influence over the criminal world depicted in the series. Mulgrew's commanding screen presence will likely add a sense of gravity to the narrative, particularly in high-stakes scenes that require a seasoned performer.

Ving Rhames joins the cast as Bart, a character whose experience and wisdom could serve as either guidance or a warning for Ray. Rhames has a long history in crime and action films, with notable roles in the *Mission: Impossible* franchise and *Pulp Fiction*. His inclusion in *Dope Thief* suggests that his character may play a mentor-like role or act as a formidable antagonist.

Other notable cast members include Amir Arison as Mark Nader, Dustin Nguyen as Son Pham, and Nesta Cooper as Michelle. Each of these actors contributes to the intricate web of relationships that define the world of *Dope Thief*. Their performances help build a layered and dynamic environment where every character has a stake in the unfolding events.

Character development is a crucial aspect of *Dope Thief*, as the story explores themes of loyalty, betrayal, and survival. The choices made by Ray and Manny are influenced by the people around them, making the supporting cast an essential part of the narrative. The interactions between these characters help shape the moral dilemmas and conflicts that drive the story forward. The performances must capture the tension and emotional weight that define the world of *Dope Thief*, ensuring that audiences remain engaged from beginning to end.

The production of the series was not without its challenges, particularly in terms of casting changes and behind-the-scenes conflicts.

Initially, Michael Mando was cast in a key role but was later replaced by Wagner Moura due to an on-set altercation. Such changes can significantly impact the development of a character, requiring adjustments in performance and storytelling. The shift from Mando to Moura brought a different energy to the role, potentially altering the dynamics between characters in ways that could enhance the overall narrative.

Filming took place in Philadelphia, a location that adds authenticity to the crime drama's setting. The city's urban landscape provides a gritty and realistic backdrop that complements the tone of the story. The production process, however, faced delays due to industry-wide strikes, leading to pauses in filming. These challenges required the cast and crew to adapt, ensuring that the final product maintained its intended quality despite unforeseen obstacles.

The casting decisions and performances in *Dope Thief* are central to its success as a crime drama. Each actor brings a unique presence that enhances the storytelling, making the characters feel real and compelling. The chemistry between Brian Tyree Henry and Wagner Moura will be particularly significant, as their relationship drives the central conflict of the series. The supporting cast adds layers of complexity, ensuring that the story remains engaging and multi-dimensional.

Chapter 2

Production & Development

Bringing *Dope Thief* to the screen was a process that involved a creative blend of literary adaptation, industry expertise, and logistical coordination. The television miniseries is based on Dennis Tafoya's 2009 novel of the same name, a gripping crime drama that captivated readers with its intense storytelling and complex characters. The journey from novel to screen required a vision that could translate the raw intensity of the book into a compelling visual narrative. This responsibility fell primarily on Peter Craig, who served as the series' creator and writer. Craig, known for his work on major productions, ensured that the thematic depth of the novel was preserved while also making necessary adjustments to fit the format of a television series. His ability to maintain the essence of the original work while adapting it for a modern audience was instrumental in shaping *Dope Thief* into what it has become.

A crucial aspect of the series' development was the involvement of key industry figures behind the scenes. Ridley Scott, a highly respected filmmaker with a track record of producing visually stunning and narratively complex films, served as an executive producer and directed the pilot episode. His reputation for meticulous craftsmanship and cinematic storytelling provided *Dope Thief* with an authoritative creative direction. Alongside Scott, other executive producers, including David W. Zucker, Jordan Sheehan, Clayton Krueger, and Brian Tyree Henry, contributed to ensuring that the series maintained a high production standard. Their combined experience in television and film production played a critical role in establishing *Dope Thief* as a polished and compelling crime drama.

Filming locations were carefully selected to bring authenticity to the story. Given that the plot is set in Philadelphia, it was crucial for production to capture the city's distinctive atmosphere. The series was primarily filmed in and around Philadelphia, with various urban and suburban settings chosen to reflect the gritty and immersive world of the novel. The authenticity of the locations added depth to the storytelling, making the setting feel as much a part of the narrative as the characters themselves. However, filming in real urban settings presented logistical challenges, including coordinating with city officials, managing traffic disruptions, and dealing with unpredictable weather conditions. Despite these obstacles, the production team remained committed to maintaining the realism necessary to enhance the overall viewing experience.

During production, the series underwent a significant transformation with its title change. Originally, *Dope Thief* was developed under the title *Sinking Spring*, a reference that had its own thematic significance. However, in November 2024, it was officially announced that the title had been reverted to *Dope Thief*, aligning it more closely with the novel. This decision was likely made to reinforce the connection between the source material and the adaptation, ensuring that audiences familiar with the book would immediately recognize the project. The title change also helped set expectations for the tone and themes of the series, emphasizing its crime drama roots and the focus on deception, heists, and consequences.

One of the most significant disruptions during the production process was the Writers Guild of America strike, which affected many projects across the industry. *Dope Thief* was no exception, as filming was temporarily halted on May 9, 2023, due to the strike. The delay impacted the production schedule, leading to adjustments in planning and execution. Strikes of this nature often create uncertainty in the industry, as negotiations between writers and studios can take time to resolve. The team behind *Dope Thief* had to navigate these challenges while ensuring that the integrity of the project remained intact. Once the strike concluded, production resumed with renewed focus, allowing the series to progress toward its planned release date.

Despite these hurdles, *Dope Thief* remained on track, and its premiere was officially set for March 14, 2025. The resilience of the production team and the dedication of the cast and crew played a crucial role in overcoming obstacles. Every stage of development, from securing a strong creative team to managing on-set challenges, contributed to shaping *Dope Thief* into a compelling crime drama that is poised to engage audiences. The journey from novel to screen was not without its difficulties, but through a combination of talent, strategic decision-making, and perseverance, the series was successfully brought to life.

Chapter 3

Plot, Themes & Possible Twists

The narrative of *Dope Thief* revolves around crime, deception, and the inevitable consequences that follow. The story follows two lifelong friends who pose as DEA agents to rob drug dealers, a dangerous scheme that puts them in the crosshairs of both law enforcement and the criminal underworld. Their elaborate heists initially appear successful, but the deeper they go, the more they realize they are in over their heads. As tensions rise and alliances are tested, the protagonists must navigate a world where trust is a luxury they cannot afford. Their journey is marked by high-stakes encounters, betrayals, and moral dilemmas that challenge their perception of loyalty and survival. The series builds suspense by gradually unraveling the layers of deception, forcing the characters to confront the consequences of their actions in a world where one wrong move can mean the difference between life and death.

A central theme of *Dope Thief* is the dynamic between friendship and betrayal. The bond between the main characters is both their greatest strength and their biggest vulnerability. Their shared history and deep trust make them effective partners, but as their circumstances become more dangerous, their loyalty is tested. The pressures of their criminal activities reveal cracks in their relationship, leading to moments of doubt, fear, and inevitable betrayals. The tension between personal loyalty and self-preservation becomes a driving force in the story, shaping the decisions they make and the paths they choose. This exploration of friendship under extreme circumstances adds emotional depth to the narrative, making the characters' struggles more compelling and relatable.

The contrast between law and morality is another significant theme in *Dope Thief*. The protagonists operate outside the legal system, yet their actions raise ethical questions about justice and survival. Their impersonation of law enforcement officers blurs the line between right and wrong, challenging traditional notions of morality. While their crimes are undeniably illegal, their motivations and personal struggles make them complex figures rather than outright villains. The series invites viewers to question where the boundaries of justice lie and whether moral compromises are ever justified. This exploration of ethical ambiguity adds complexity to the storyline, making it more than just a standard crime drama.

Survival in the criminal underworld is a recurring theme that shapes the characters' choices and development. The world they navigate is ruthless, where power shifts quickly and alliances are fragile. Every decision they make carries consequences, and the constant threat of violence forces them to adapt or face deadly repercussions. The tension between ambition and self-preservation drives much of the plot, creating a sense of urgency and unpredictability. The series does not romanticize crime but rather portrays the harsh realities of life in a world where trust is rare and survival is never guaranteed. This unflinching look at the criminal underworld sets *Dope Thief* apart from more stylized portrayals of crime, grounding it in a realism that heightens the stakes.

The story introduces several potential plot twists that keep audiences engaged. Unexpected betrayals, shifting allegiances, and hidden agendas create an atmosphere of constant suspense. Characters who appear trustworthy may have their own hidden motives, and seemingly minor details may lead to shocking revelations. The unpredictability of the plot ensures that viewers are kept on edge, never quite sure what will happen next. Unanswered questions add to the intrigue, leaving room for speculation and interpretation. The ambiguity surrounding certain character decisions and plot developments allows for deeper engagement, as audiences analyze clues and predict possible outcomes.

Dope Thief distinguishes itself from other crime dramas through its character-driven storytelling, realistic portrayal of criminal life, and moral complexity. Unlike traditional crime thrillers that focus solely on action and intrigue, this series delves into the psychological and emotional struggles of its protagonists. The emphasis on character development and relationships adds a human element that makes the stakes feel more personal. Additionally, its exploration of ethical dilemmas sets it apart from more conventional narratives that present clear distinctions between heroes and villains. The gritty realism of *Dope Thief* aligns it with other critically acclaimed crime dramas, but its unique approach to storytelling and character dynamics ensures that it stands out in the genre.

Chapter 4

Critical Reception & Audience Expectations

The anticipation surrounding *Dope Thief* has been significant, with early reviews and critical reception offering insight into its potential impact. As the release date of March 14, 2025, approaches, industry experts, critics, and general audiences have already begun forming expectations based on trailers, production details, and early screenings. Platforms such as Rotten Tomatoes, Metacritic, and IMDb have provided initial ratings that reflect both critical acclaim and audience interest. The reception of the series among critics has been largely positive, with praise directed at its compelling storytelling, strong performances, and realistic depiction of crime and moral dilemmas. The balance of action, drama, and psychological depth has set *Dope Thief* apart from conventional crime thrillers, earning it comparisons to some of the most highly regarded series in the genre.

Critics have highlighted several aspects that contribute to the success of *Dope Thief*, including the nuanced performances of its lead actors. Brian Tyree Henry and Wagner Moura have been lauded for their chemistry and ability to bring complexity to their characters. Their portrayal of two criminals navigating the dangerous consequences of their actions has been described as both intense and emotionally compelling. The character development throughout the series is another aspect that has received acclaim, as it avoids stereotypical crime drama tropes in favor of deeper explorations of friendship, trust, and survival. Reviewers have also praised the cinematography and production quality, emphasizing how the use of real locations and gritty visuals enhances the authenticity of the story. The directing style, particularly under the guidance of Ridley Scott as the executive producer, has been noted for its ability to create a tense and immersive atmosphere.

While *Dope Thief* has garnered significant praise, some critics have pointed out areas where the series could have been stronger. One of the most common critiques revolves around the pacing of certain episodes. Some reviewers feel that while the series excels in building tension and character depth, there are moments where the pacing slows down, potentially affecting engagement for audiences expecting a more fast-paced crime thriller. Additionally, a few critics have noted that certain plot developments, while compelling, may feel familiar to fans of the genre. However, these critiques have not overshadowed the overall positive reception, as most reviewers acknowledge the series' ability to distinguish itself through its unique character dynamics and morally complex narrative.

The audience response to *Dope Thief* has been equally enthusiastic, with significant anticipation leading up to its release. Social media discussions, fan theories, and online forums have been filled with speculation about plot twists, character arcs, and potential surprises in the storyline. The casting choices, particularly the inclusion of established actors with strong dramatic backgrounds, have generated excitement among viewers who appreciate performances that bring depth to crime dramas. The involvement of Ridley Scott as an executive producer has also contributed to heightened expectations, as his reputation for delivering high-quality productions has reassured audiences of the series' potential success. The fact that the series is based on a well-regarded novel has also fueled interest, with fans of the book eager to see how the adaptation remains faithful to or diverges from the original material.

Comparisons to other Apple TV+ originals have also influenced audience expectations. Apple TV+ has developed a reputation for producing high-caliber series across various genres, with crime dramas such as *Black Bird* and *Slow Horses* receiving widespread acclaim. The success of these shows has set a high standard, and *Dope Thief* is expected to meet or exceed the bar established by its predecessors. Viewers familiar with Apple TV+ content anticipate a production that combines compelling storytelling with cinematic quality, reinforcing their eagerness to see how *Dope Thief* measures up. The series' potential to carve out a unique identity within the crime drama genre will be a key factor in determining its long-term impact and staying power.

Chapter 5

Everything You Need to Know Before Watching

The anticipation surrounding *Dope Thief* has only grown as its release approaches. With an intriguing premise, a strong cast, and the backing of Apple TV+, this crime drama promises to deliver an engaging experience for viewers who appreciate character-driven storytelling and high-stakes narratives. Before diving into the series, there are several key aspects to consider that will enhance the viewing experience and set expectations appropriately. Understanding the core themes, critical reception, and what the series aims to achieve will help audiences appreciate the depth of the story and the complexity of its characters.

This book has explored various elements of *Dope Thief*, from its source material and production to the themes that drive its narrative. One of the key takeaways is the series' commitment to portraying crime in a way that goes beyond action and suspense. At its core, *Dope Thief* is a story about deception, trust, and the consequences of one's actions. The protagonists, who engage in high-stakes heists by impersonating DEA agents, are not just criminals but deeply flawed individuals navigating a world where survival depends on quick thinking and resilience. The show does not glorify their actions but instead explores the emotional and psychological weight of their decisions.

Another significant takeaway is the moral ambiguity that shapes the storyline. Unlike traditional crime dramas that focus on clear distinctions between good and evil, *Dope Thief* presents a world where those lines are blurred. The audience is encouraged to empathize with characters whose choices may be legally wrong but are driven by desperation, ambition, or circumstances beyond their control. This approach allows for a more layered narrative that challenges conventional perspectives on justice and morality.

The performances of Brian Tyree Henry and Wagner Moura add further depth to the series, bringing authenticity and emotional intensity to their roles. Their chemistry and ability to convey the struggles of their characters contribute significantly to the show's impact. The direction and cinematography also enhance the storytelling, using visuals to create an immersive atmosphere that reflects the tension and unpredictability of the criminal underworld.

With these elements in mind, the question arises as to whether *Dope Thief* is worth watching. The answer depends on what viewers seek in a crime drama. Those who appreciate fast-paced action and straightforward storytelling may find some elements of the series slower or more introspective than expected. However, for audiences who enjoy character-driven narratives with complex themes and moral dilemmas, *Dope Thief* offers a compelling and thought-provoking experience. The show's ability to balance suspense with emotional depth makes it stand out from more conventional crime dramas, and its emphasis on psychological realism provides a fresh perspective on the genre.

The quality of the production also contributes to its appeal. Apple TV+ has consistently delivered high-caliber series, and *Dope Thief* is no exception. With strong writing, meticulous attention to detail, and a commitment to authenticity, the series maintains a level of craftsmanship that enhances its storytelling. The involvement of Ridley Scott as an executive producer further reinforces its credibility, as his expertise in creating visually striking and narratively rich content ensures a high standard of execution.

The show's appeal extends to a wide range of viewers. Fans of crime dramas such as *Breaking Bad*, *Ozark*, and *Black Bird* will likely find *Dope Thief* engaging due to its focus on flawed characters navigating dangerous situations. Those who appreciate narratives that explore human psychology, ethical dilemmas, and the consequences of deception will also find much to appreciate in the series. Additionally, viewers who enjoy intense performances and strong character dynamics will be drawn to the chemistry between the lead actors.

For those new to the crime drama genre, *Dope Thief* provides an accessible yet gripping introduction. While it contains the tension and intrigue expected from crime stories, its emphasis on emotional depth and personal struggles sets it apart. The series does not rely solely on action but instead builds suspense through character development and unpredictable plot twists. This balance makes it appealing to audiences who may not typically gravitate toward crime dramas but are interested in well-crafted storytelling.

The success of *Dope Thief* may also influence the future of crime drama adaptations. The genre has evolved over the years, with modern crime dramas placing greater emphasis on character psychology and thematic depth. The trend of exploring morally complex protagonists and ethically ambiguous situations has resonated with audiences, leading to more nuanced storytelling in television and film. If *Dope Thief* receives strong critical and audience reception, it could encourage more adaptations that focus on character-driven narratives rather than solely action-oriented plots.

Streaming platforms like Apple TV+, Netflix, and HBO Max have become major players in the production of high-quality crime dramas, and the success of *Dope Thief* could further reinforce the demand for sophisticated storytelling within the genre. The rise of limited series as a storytelling format has allowed for more in-depth character exploration, and *Dope Thief* fits well within this trend. Its potential impact on future crime dramas may be seen in how creators approach character development, pacing, and thematic exploration in upcoming projects.

Conclusion

As the release of *Dope Thief* approaches, audiences have the opportunity to experience a crime drama that goes beyond action and suspense. This series is built on a foundation of strong storytelling, well-developed characters, and deep themes that explore trust, betrayal, and the consequences of choices. It is more than just a story about crime—it is about human nature and survival in a world where every decision has a cost.

This book has provided a detailed look at what makes *Dope Thief* unique, from its complex characters to its moral dilemmas and unexpected twists. By understanding these elements, viewers will be better prepared to fully appreciate the series when it premieres. Knowing what to expect allows for a deeper connection to the story and its themes, making the viewing experience even more engaging.

As you get ready to watch, keep in mind that *Dope Thief* will challenge perspectives on justice, loyalty, and survival. It is a series that invites audiences to think critically while being entertained by its gripping plot and emotional depth. Whether you are a longtime fan of crime dramas or new to the genre, this series has the potential to leave a lasting impression.

With all the anticipation surrounding its release, *Dope Thief* is set to be one of the most talked-about crime dramas of the year. Prepare to be drawn into a world of deception, danger, and moral complexity. The journey is about to begin.

Printed in Dunstable, United Kingdom